Take Control of Your Thoughts

Pulling Down Strongholds in Your Mind

by
Dr. Donald Shorter

Harrison House
Tulsa, Oklahoma

Unless otherwise indicated, all Scripture quotations are taken from the *King James Version* of the Bible.

12 11 10 09   20 19 18 17 16 15 14 13 12 11

Take Control of Your Thoughts—
Pulling Down Strongholds in Your Mind
ISBN 13: 978-1-57794-606-9
ISBN 10: 1-57794-606-5
Copyright © 2003 by Don Shorter Ministries
P.O. Box 44800
Tacoma, WA 98444

Published by Harrison House, Inc.
P. O. Box 35035
Tulsa, Oklahoma 74153

Printed in the United States of America.

Contents

Introduction

Every person goes through change, either negative or positive. Change is always occurring. To grow and become more effective for the Kingdom of God, positive change must occur.

When you are born again (become a Christian), you experience a spiritual change instantaneously. This is done by asking Jesus to be Lord of your life and accepting Him as your Lord and Savior, according to Romans 10:9-10. The Word of God simply says that if anyone will confess Jesus as Lord of his life and believe that God raised Jesus from the dead, he will be saved. Once that's done, you are *born* into God's kingdom, and you become a child of God.

The Bible declares that when you become a Christian, you are a new creature: "... behold, all things are become new" (2 Cor. 5:17). You pass from death to life immediately. (John 5:24.) However, there are two areas that do not immediately change: 1) your soul (your mind, will, and emotions), and 2) your physical body (the flesh). These become two of the hottest battlegrounds in your life. As your relationship with God grows, it will be more and more evident that your "soulish" part (the mind, will, and emotions) is the enemy's *focal point* of attack. In this book we will learn how to overcome in these two areas through God's Word.

When we accept Jesus as Lord and Savior, we are actually born of the Holy Spirit. (John 3:5,6,8.) At this point our lives take on new meaning. We have a new outlook on life and a new Lord to serve. The Apostle Paul stated it this way:

> **For I delight in the law of God after the inward man,**
>
> **But I see another law in my members, warring against the law of my mind, and bringing me into captivity to the law of sin which is in my members.**
>
> **O wretched man that I am! Who shall deliver me from the body of this death?**
>
> **I thank God through Jesus Christ our Lord....**
>
> **Romans 7:22-25**

Jesus is our Deliverer.

Two laws are at work within us. Our "inward man," or spirit man, delights or seeks after the law of God. The war against the law of our mind is waged in the mind of the believer, as well as the unbeliever, 24 hours per day, 7 days per week, 365 days per year.

Thank God the believer's mind can be settled through the Spirit of God (the Holy Spirit) and faith in the Word of God.

God Our Deliverer

Our bodies naturally desire to fulfill the lusts of the world, while our recreated human spirits desire to go the way of God. In the Bible Paul says that God will deliver us from this dilemma through Jesus Christ our Lord.

In 2 Corinthians 10:3-5, the warfare we wage in our mind is further explained by Paul:

For though we walk in the flesh, we do not war after the flesh:

(For the weapons of our warfare are not carnal, but mighty through God to the pulling down of strongholds;)

Casting down imaginations, and every high thing that exalteth itself against the knowledge of God, and bringing into captivity every thought to the obedience of Christ.

In verses 4 and 5, we will begin to see and understand the strategy God has given us in His Word to win the battle for control of our soul. Throughout this book we will examine an effective process designed to have the proper weapons deployed at any given time in our life to help us cast down negative imaginations and bring every thought into obedience to Christ. Our weapons are given to us by God, as Ephesians 6:14-17 says:

Stand therefore, having your loins girt about with truth, and having on the breastplate of righteousness;

And your feet shod with the preparation of the gospel of peace;

Above all, taking the shield of faith, wherewith ye shall be able to quench all the fiery darts of the wicked.

And take the helmet of salvation, and the sword of the Spirit, which is the word of God.

Our main focus in this book will be on the sword of the Spirit, which is the Word of God. We will then become equipped to analyze any thought that exalts itself above the knowledge of God and His best for our life. By doing this we will find that every thought will become naked and open for our examination.

Hebrews 4:12-13 says: "For the *Word of God* is quick [living, alive], and powerful, and sharper than any twoedged sword, piercing even to the dividing asunder of soul and spirit, and of the joints and marrow, and is a discerner of the thoughts and intents of the heart. Neither is there any creature that is not manifest in His sight: But all things are naked and opened unto the eyes of him with whom we have to do."

1

We Are Redeemed From the Curse

Many believers mistakenly believe that once they are born again they are no longer a target for the enemy, but that isn't true. To better understand, consider this example. When a wild animal is born in the forest, the job of the parents is to protect and feed this newborn creature every moment of its very early existence. The forest is filled with nourishment as well as predators, waiting for an opportunity to take advantage of the carelessness of the parents or the curiosity of the newborn. Many may say, "It's a jungle out there," but in reality, it's just warfare in the day-to-day lifestyle in the animal kingdom. Let's look at that from a spiritual viewpoint for our lives.

Adam's transgression (Gen. 3:17) caused the world, including man and woman, to be cursed, creating in many ways a jungle. Now the word *curse* means nothing good at all. However, as believers, we are redeemed from that curse by the blood of Jesus.

> **Christ hath redeemed us from the curse of the law, being made a curse for us:**
>
> **for it is written, Cursed is every one that hangeth on a tree:**
>
> **That the blessing of Abraham might come on the Gentiles through Jesus Christ; that we might receive the promise of the Spirit through faith.**
>
> **Galatians 3:13,14**

Believers are blessed (fortunate, to be envied) because they are no longer under a curse.

Jesus became that curse and died on the cross to redeem us from the sins of the world. But that did not take away the curse for the entire world. It was only for those living in the world who accept His sacrifice on the cross. This means we must daily deal with those of the world still under the influence of the curse, even though we are personally redeemed from it ourselves.

God has given us weapons to win the battle against the enemy in the jungle out there. It's up to us to learn how to use them.

God's Weapons Are Mightier

Satan is known as the god of this world, and he tries to come after us with his weapons. However, as we just read in 2 Corinthians 10:4-5, these weapons given to believers are not carnal (of this world), but are mighty through God with a definite purpose—to pull down the enemy's strongholds.

Verse 5 talks about casting down certain things. Before we can cast down anything, we must know the authority we have to cast down these high things that exalt themselves above the knowledge of God (His will and purpose in our lives).

This passage states that the weapons to which every believer has access are mighty. We are only mighty through God, not through ourselves or the might of others.

To further understand this concept, I must explain that the will of God is expressed in the Word of God, the Bible. The Bible must become the final authority on any subject in life as well as the guide for casting down or exalting anything. We Christians must examine our environment in relationship to our faith in God's Word to understand His will for our life. Just as the newborn creature of the forest, we must rely upon the heavenly Father to discern what is helpful or harmful and to focus on His will as expressed in His Word.

For some Christians this process does not begin properly. Religious traditions, sectarian barriers, or the cares of this world stop them from being fed or led by God's Word. They are soon confused, frustrated, and defeated. With that mindset they become instant lunch for their enemy, falling prey to his wicked vices and devices, and are slowly absorbed back into the jungle of this world as Satan's trophies.

For other Christians the process begins quickly, only to stop at a certain level of growth because they feel they have matured spiritually or materially. To assure continued spiritual growth, we must continue to learn in every situation how to cast down the thoughts that Satan presents to our minds and exalt the Word.

Your Life Is Being Shaped

Information, opinions, teachings, doctrines, arguments, or lifestyles will shape the life and habits of any person. From birth, we immediately begin to be shaped by those around us. All of these influences must be analyzed, sorted, accepted, rejected, or replaced. All work as building blocks in our growth.

There is no difference when we are spiritually born again. The input we receive will determine our growth in every aspect of life.

I remember the conception and birth of each of our children. Each time, as soon as my wife and I learned that she was pregnant, we began praying, speaking life to our baby while it was only days into conception in my wife's womb. We would begin telling each child they were blessed, smart, prosperous, and healthy according to the Word of God, even though my wife was only days or weeks past conception. We continued throughout the pregnancy until each child was born already shaped in the words of faith spoken before they were ever seen.

Death and life are in the power of the tongue....

Proverbs 18:21

You live or die by the words you receive, accept, and exalt over your life, as well as the words you speak over your life.

Every day we are presented with hundreds of thoughts, ideas, and suggestions. For example, today you could hear or read a number of suggestions from billboards, signs, bumper stickers, radio, television, and telephone propositions, as well as past memories and images of the future. *You* will decide what to believe and exalt in your life. You alone control this part of your life. God gave you the authority and control over this area; you are the determining factor. All of these influences are consistently in the process of suggesting things to the human imagination, some good and some detrimental to your growth as a mature person and as a successful Christian.

To live a successful Christian life, your state of mind must be checked constantly to allow you to receive the information needed to operate effectively in today's society. This cannot be accomplished by living life with your senses closed off. You must understand that you will be presented with negative information regardless of how holy and sanctified you are. The key to living victoriously is to remember that your thoughts are controlled by the input you allow to be received and accepted as truth and exalted as the standards in your life.

In Proverbs 23:7, we read that a person is determined by his thoughts.

> For as he thinketh in his heart, so is he....
> The Bible also says of Jesus,
> ... as he is, so are we in this world.

> 1 John 4:17

Catch hold of this truth and never forget it: To be presented with a thought, suggestion, or idea is one thing; but what you do with that thought, suggestion, or idea is totally different. It determines your entire future physically, mentally, and spiritually. Remember, you are the deciding factor. It is your decision to accept or reject these thoughts. *Decision Time*

Years ago, my wife and I became hooked on soap operas and opened ourselves up to be trained in a lifestyle we did not want. Over time, we somewhat lived the lives of the TV characters. Many Christians do not understand why following the lives of people living a lifestyle of sin on television can negatively affect their lives. We did not know until our eyes were refocused on the Word of God.

I once heard someone say that the person I become within the next few years is determined by the books I read, the things I listen to, and the people I associate with today. *WOW!!*

7

He that walketh with wise men shall be wise,
but a companion of fools shall be destroyed.

Proverbs 13:20

Make no friendship with an angry man; and
with a furious man thou shalt not go,

Lest thou learn his ways, and get a snare to
thy soul.

Proverbs 22:24,25

As I began to look over my life and compare it to
the Word of God and His will for me, I noticed that
my activities during my young Christian life were all
on a very negative basis in comparison to the
lifestyle (conversation) described in the Word of
God. I also began to understand that I was being
snared and destroyed. No one had told me that it is
Satan who destroys. I thought (because I was taught
at a church I went to) that it was God just putting
me through test after test to make me strong (even
though I was getting weaker by the minute). Little
did I know that I was agreeing to destroy myself by
listening to and studying Satan's lifestyle and allowing him to train my mind, choose the words of my
mouth, and ultimately control my deeds.

...walk not as other Gentiles walk, in the
vanity of their mind.

Ephesians 4:17

Notice, there is supposed to be a difference in the walk (daily lifestyle) of the believer versus the unbeliever. The Greek word for Gentile means a person without God and with no hope in the world. However, the walk for both the believer and unbeliever begins in the mind, determining the direction of the person's walk toward God's will or away from God's will.

As believers, we are to be aware of our state of mind at all times. In our daily walk, as we receive information from the world, we must have a different state of mind.

God's Army

In 2 Timothy 2:4, Paul writes to Timothy:

No man that warreth entangleth himself with the affairs of this life; that he may please him who hath chosen him to be a soldier.

Once we are born again, we are automatically inducted into the army of the Lord. We are commanded to not become entangled in the affairs of this world. That doesn't mean we do not live in the world. It simply means we must remember who we are while we are in it. You are a soldier chosen by

God and on duty 24 hours a day. Make a decision to learn who you are in God's army and how to use His weapons to receive the victory Jesus has won for us.

Begin by reading, studying, praying, watching programs, and listening to tapes about who you are in Christ. Most of all, join a Bible-teaching church that will help you know who you are in Christ. Your life will begin to take a turn for the better as you begin to apply the principles of God's Word in your life.

My people are destroyed for lack of knowledge....

Hosea 4:6

Knowledge of God's law (His Word) is so important to ensure victory for you. If you don't learn to exalt God's law, Satan will force his law upon you.

2

How You See Yourself

So far, we have established that everyone is presented with negative information. Now, let's look at 2 Corinthians 10:5 again, but let's focus on the word "imaginations."

Casting down imaginations, and every high thing that exalteth itself against the knowledge of God, and bringing into captivity every thought to the obedience of Christ.

Genesis 1:27 states that God created man in His own image. As a result, man became the highest being created on the earth. He was made a little lower than the angels. The word *imagination* can be broken down this way, *image-a-nation*. We read earlier in Proverbs 23:7 that as a man "thinketh in his heart, so is he." This has to do with the imagination of a person. The image of a person is one of the most important indicators of growth in his or her relationship with God. Along with this self-concept is the view of self-worth and general belief in success. How you imagine yourself determines whether you please God or not and whether or not you will be successful in life according to the Bible.

God's View of Man

In Numbers 13:33, the children of Israel were faced with entering Canaan and taking what God had said belonged to them. God had called the children of Israel strong and courageous, and had told them that He had given them the land of their enemies that flowed with milk and honey. He had said that it was a good land and that as His children, they should have it; that He would fight for them and they were to go and take the land He had promised them.

If God said it, His promise had to be fulfilled because God cannot lie. However, the children of Israel imagined themselves as grasshoppers, entirely different from the way God had imagined them or spoken of them. According to Scripture, they saw themselves as grasshoppers, and because of this poor self-image and self-pity, they were grasshoppers in their enemies' sight as well.

And there we saw the giants, the sons of Anak, which come of the giants: and we were in our own sight as grasshoppers, and so we were in their sight.

Numbers 13:33

This view began in their mind and reflected what they thought of themselves, not how God saw them or spoke of them. God called them His children. He had not made grasshoppers of His sons and daughters created in His own image!

This negative view displeased the Lord and caused the Israelites to wander on a 40-year trail, murmuring against God and His chosen leaders. Ironically, this Scripture clearly shows who started the name-calling. It was not the enemies of God. It was the children of God who first considered themselves as grasshoppers and spoke what was in their hearts. When you do this, it makes it so easy for your enemies to agree and set your words into motion.

Your Self-Image

How you imagine yourself as a believer is very important. It determines how others think of you and whether or not you please God. So many times we hear people talk about working on their self-image.

The only true way for anyone to work on that is to look at the Creator of all mankind. God, our Father, through our Lord Jesus Christ, in whose image man was made, is our Creator. (Col. 1:15.) Any image or imagination of yourself that is not based on the Word of God is incorrect.

As a believer it is important for you to know who you are in Christ. You must be ready at all times to receive words said about you that concur with the Word of God, as well as cast down any imagination about yourself that is not according to God's Word. The Bible is your guide for your self-image.

To receive more abundantly from God, speak and exalt His Word. The Holy Spirit working in you will prosper your words so your faith becomes sight. Begin to meditate and picture what God's Word says about you and what you can do in Christ.

Unchecked Thoughts

It's important to learn to cast down any unchecked thoughts about past failures or successes that are diametrically opposed to the Word of God. They are potentially dangerous to our spiritual well-being.

"what if something negative happens"

For many Christians, the idea of something negative happening to them has the ability to paralyze them in such a way as to give place to fear. If not cast down, these negative thoughts or imaginations will return again and again, holding the victim prisoner in his own mind. The root cause of worry is fear, and the root cause of fear is an *unchecked imagination* and lack of knowledge of the Word of God.

Second Timothy 1:7 states, "For God hath not given us the spirit of fear; but of power, and of love, and of a sound mind." If God gives a sound mind, then Satan, who is opposed to God, must be the one who is giving the spirit of fear. You must make the decision to arrest negative thoughts and cast them down by the Word of God. God has given you the authority to do so.

Carnality

For the weapons of our warfare are not carnal....

2 Corinthians 10:4

That word "carnal" needs to be explained. Have you ever heard of "chili con carne"? The word "carne" is related to carnal, meaning meat or flesh. The weapons of our warfare are not carnal, or of the flesh. They are not according to our brain power or intellect with the ability relying on the physical senses ("I'll figure this one out myself"). Neither are they of the feelings of the flesh ("I feel victorious"). Rather, they are "mighty through God to the pulling down of strongholds." God has given you mighty spiritual weapons; they are not carnal. To live victoriously you must understand how to use them.

Ruled by the Law of Lasciviousness

Who being past feeling have given themselves over unto lasciviousness, to work all uncleanness with greediness.

Ephesians 4:19

When carnal efforts are in the forefront of the battles of a born-again person, the ultimate state of existence and lifestyle are based on lawlessness. Lawlessness (or taking your life into your own hands) is the spirit of the world. The Bible clearly calls this attitude lasciviousness. This word, however, cannot be applied to a person who is not born again, because people of the world do what they want without restraint, by the very nature of their existence. However, when this carnal state of mind controls a believer's life, allowing certain habits and behaviors to continue, this unchecked state of existence is considered lasciviousness. Simply defined, it means a lack of restraint, first in thoughts, then in words, and ultimately in deeds. Thoughts are seeds, and seeds are going to come up someday if they are planted consistently in the right conditions. If a person continues to put the wrong things in his or her body (drugs, alcohol, unhealthy foods), eventually the negative effects will surface.

Everyone has certain weaknesses of the flesh that Satan is aware of. For some, it may be a chemical dependency on drugs or alcohol. For others, it may be lust or the love of money. Whatever the weakness, it's important to understand that God has given us weapons to use to combat things working against us. Those desires left unchecked will cause that person to continue living life in a state of mind ruled by lasciviousness. Some Christians are totally out of control—either in their finances, bodies, homes, or imaginations. They may have accepted Christ and may be going to heaven but have no control over their lives.

The opposite of lasciviousness is excellence. Excellence says, "I am not going to put up with sloppiness, laziness, and lack of constraint. I am not going to have those kinds of negative thoughts ruling my life." Only you, the believer, can break the power of the devil over your thoughts. What will it be, excellence or lasciviousness? You choose.

Thoughts Must Be Planted First

Satan desires to bombard your mind through every means possible, such as the media and the Internet. However, without the incubation process of negative imaginations and thoughts, he cannot effectively cause your life to be changed by these bombardments. Satan can't put you in a neck hold and pull you down to a bar and get you drunk. He first suggests the idea. He may use anyone, perhaps someone you believe is a friend. Keep in mind, the thought must first be planted. Many Christians silently deal with areas of temptation and bombardment in their minds, while trying to hide them from people around them.

Remember, 2 Corinthians 10 states that the weapons of our warfare are not carnal. We are in a war, and the enemy is constantly trying to attack his opponents. This is you if you are on God's side. The only way to win the battle against our opponent is to remember that when it comes to regulating the thoughts in our minds, we must learn to compare everything—thought, word, or deed—with the Word of God. Anything below the standard of the Word must be immediately cast down.

Imaginations and perceptions are very powerful. We see this in children who watch a steady diet of Saturday morning cartoons. They see themselves in the image placed in their minds by television. This occurs not only with children, but adults as well. For 15 years I worked in the media, particularly television and radio, and I've seen the effect that imagination and perceptions has had upon well-meaning people. The media effectively uses the power of suggestion to its advantage to make a profit and sell ideas, concepts, services, and lifestyles to anyone who will listen. Many find themselves meditating or muttering the ideas, concepts, or logo of someone's company without any conscious thought.

The media has a tremendous influence on us, but I'm not saying that we should be paranoid about everything in the media or that everything in it is satanically derived. But I know first-hand how imaginations can be used to change habits and lifestyles through suggesting an idea at just the right time.

Look at Genesis 2:17. God is speaking very clear instructions to Adam regarding the trees of the garden:

> But of the tree of the knowledge of good and evil, thou shalt not eat of it: for in the day that thou eatest thereof thou shalt surely die.

In Genesis 3:1 the serpent, Satan, is speaking, questioning Eve about what God told Adam:

> Now the serpent was more subtle than any beast of the field which the Lord God had made. And he said unto the woman, Yea, *hath God said*, Ye shall not eat of every tree of the garden?

Two things are wrong with the interrogation. Why is the serpent asking Eve what God said? She was not there; Adam was. Second why is the serpent questioning God? It was certainly not for more clarification. These are two very important keys.

> And the woman said unto the serpent, We may eat of the fruit of the trees of the garden:

> But of the fruit of the tree which is in the midst of the garden, God hath said, Ye shall not eat of it, neither shall ye touch it, lest ye die.

God did not say, "You shall not touch it, lest you die." Eve misunderstood. In verse 4, notice this:

> And the serpent said unto the woman, Ye shall not surely die.

Now go back to Genesis 2:16-17:

> And the Lord God commanded the man, saying, Of every tree of the garden thou mayest freely eat:
> But of the tree of the knowledge of good and evil, thou shalt not eat of it: for in the day that thou eatest thereof thou shalt surely die.

Satan is the liar here, as always. The distortion of the truth will always be Satan's tactic to steal blessings from you. The enemy cannot steal outright anything from you without your permission. He must deceive you out of what God has given you for you to lose it, either through ignorance of God's Word, or not applying the Word that you do know.

There are consequences of not knowing what God really said and what He meant in saying it.

> And when the woman saw that the tree was good for food, and that it was pleasant to the

> eyes, and a tree to be desired to make one wise,
> she took of the fruit thereof, and did eat....
>
> **Genesis 3:6**

Clearly this Scripture shows that the woman began to imagine or see new ideas. This was against the knowing of God or the knowledge of God's Word spoken directly to Adam. By following this idea and allowing it to be exalted in the perception of her mind, Eve and her husband were separated from their former relationship with God.

Satan's plan is to keep us in a negative state of mind for three main reasons: guilt, condemnation, and separation from God. He wants to keep us wrapped up in our own circumstances and problems. You must begin to analyze every word and determine if it exalts itself above the knowledge of God. What you allow to enter your mind, heart, and ears is very important. Don't let garbage be dumped on you. Learn to be always conscious of what you receive.

3

The Power That Works in You

There is a powerful force waiting inside of you. "Now unto him who is able to do exceeding abundantly above all that we ask or think, according to the power that *worketh in us*" (Eph. 3:20). "Him" means God, Jesus, the Holy Spirit. He is able. Whatever you are asking, if it is in line with God's Word, whatever your situation, whatever you are dealing with, He is able to do exceeding abundantly above that. Look at 1 Corinthians 2:9:

> ...Eye hath not seen, nor ear heard, neither have entered in the heart of man, the things which God hath prepared for them that love him.

Some Christians try to think of themselves above what the Word of God says about them. At the same time, others think way below what the Word says about them and what it promises them as children of God. Both are equally wrong.

As an example, think of the Word of God as a paved road. Those who are walking firmly on the road's surface could be considered those walking firmly on the Word of God. Unfortunately, there are always some people who still choose to walk below what the Word says about them. They live by their feelings with thoughts of worthlessness and defeat. The reason many times is based on their own unregulated thoughts allowing them to live their lives contrary to the Word of God.

Consider this: Sewer pipes are usually located underneath the ground, below the road's surface. The reason is that sewage is waste, good for nothing, and very unpleasant to deal with. Sewage is something that is no longer any good. We should not allow the sewage of the world's thinking and ways of our past to enter our minds. You may hear people saying, "God is putting this on me to humble me," or "I'll never make it, I'm just a loser," or "I'll never get ahead, I'll always be poor." None of that is true. That may be your imagination or the thoughts of others about you, but it is not what the Word of God says about you. Remember, He "is able to do exceeding abundantly above all that we ask or think."

If you were asked about your finances, what would you say? Would it be according to the Word or according to your present circumstances or someone's opinion? If you were asked about your children or your job or business, would your thoughts sink to the sewer or would they be on the road (the Word of God)?

God has given you the ability to ascend to His Word, to rise up and receive from His Word; not to live above it and certainly not below it, but in it. Walk on it. That guarantees a solid foundation for success!

The last part of this Scripture says, "...above all that we can ask or think, according to the power that worketh in us." That power is the Word of God. If God's power is what is going to do it (that is, exceed your thoughts or requests), then all you have to do is put your faith to work and believe to receive. Don't worry about it or cry about it. Receive it. Don't try to explain it away; just have faith and be ready to receive it. Expect to receive exceeding abundantly above what you are asking or thinking.

God is the One who will deliver it to you, according to His power that works in you. Don't hinder or be fearful of the power working in you. Let God's power have free reign, beginning now.

Receive God's Free Gift

Without the power of God working in you, there may be very little going on in your life. The Spirit of God is inside you, working with your thoughts and words to create the promises of God for every part of your life. Remember, the Holy Spirit is working with you and in you.

Satan knows that when someone receives the gift of the Holy Spirit, that person is equipped with supernatural power. Without the power of the Holy Spirit and faith in God's Word, it's difficult to receive God's promises. Look at your life right now and ask yourself, *What is working in me?* Is the Holy Spirit working in you, or are fear, worry, and negative thoughts working in you? You have the power to cast down those imaginations that are crowding God's promises from your mind and exalt God's knowledge in your life.

The Bible says that the Holy Spirit will guide you and lead you into all truth (John 16:13), causing you to receive from God His direction and counsel.

It is literally impossible for you to effectively block the negative thoughts that come to mind without the Holy Spirit's power, discerning, and leading. It must be done by the power of God given to you. That power must be working in you.

Every time a thought comes to mind, you must determine if the thought is in line with God's will (His Word) or not. It's confusing to say, "That's negative; I don't believe that," or "I shouldn't accept that," without a standard. The standard you use must always be the knowledge of God's Word and the assistance of the Holy Spirit to help you remember. Casting down negative thoughts and fears is one thing, but eventually you must fill that emptiness with something. Replace negative thoughts with the Word of God, not religious tradition or the opinions of others.

In the last day, that great day of the feast, Jesus stood and cried out, saying, If any man thirst, let him come unto me, and drink.

He that believeth on me, as the scripture hath said, out of his belly [heart] shall flow rivers of living water.

(But this spake he of the Spirit, which they that believe on him should receive....)

John 7:37-39

Some believe that the world's counselors are the only ones who will be able to help them. Some believe that doctors will come up with all that is needed to cure every ailment of their bodies. Thank God for doctors; however, it is the Holy Spirit we need. The Holy Spirit is the power source that God has given us to overcome every situation: body, soul, and spirit. God has given us a Helper—the Holy Spirit. In receiving Him, He will bring things to our remembrance, comfort us in every situation, and guide us into all truth. This can't be done by our own power.

You can receive the Holy Spirit by asking according to Luke 11:13. After you ask, pray as the Spirit leads according to Acts 2:4. Open your mouth and allow the Lord to fill it. Pray regularly in your new language according to Jude 20. ⟵ *Lisa*

Hearing and Obeying the Holy Spirit

God wants all of you, including your mind, will, and emotions. He wants your body, your spirit, everything you have. When you give yourself totally to Him, expect a return as promised.

God wants you all of the time. There are not many wives who would live in a relationship where they spent time with their husband only once a week, and the rest of the week he was not their husband. If they were committed, they would expect the same commitment from their husband, or vice versa. An uncommitted relationship will not last very long.

God is looking for a committed relationship in harmony with you. You control the ability to see yourself going somewhere and doing something great, or to see yourself defeated and in a rut. God has called you to do great things for Him, but it takes commitment. He has called you to do many great things, and you are the only one who can hold you back. God is not holding you back, and the devil can't because he's been stripped of that authority by Jesus.

Years ago, the only way I could start my car was by rolling it down a hill. I would put my car in gear and jump into it as it was rolling while jerking the clutch up quickly to start the engine. That was my lifestyle, and it went on for many months.

After a while I began to learn that if I was going to change my circumstances, I would have to use my faith, be committed, and believe what God said I could have according to His Word, not what I was imagining myself doing day after day. I had to develop a vision and image of change. I found a Scripture to stand on and began to confess and believe for a new car over and above the imaginations of the present. I had to imagine myself with a new car that started without being pushed.

This is a small thing now, but it wasn't small then. I had to stand on the Word, confess what I wanted, and believe I had received it all the while I was pushing my car down hill after hill. A short time later, a miracle happened. I received a brand-new car, and I did not have to push my car any longer. This car came with a 100,000-mile warranty and was showroom new. To receive the new car, I had to believe that God desired for me to receive the desires of my heart (according to Psalm 37:4). I had to cast down the thoughts of pushing my car any longer, and I had to see myself driving my old car to the dealership and driving off with a brand-new car.

Soon the Holy Spirit directed me to go to a certain new car dealer I had known years earlier. By the Lord's direction, I drove onto the lot and left that old clunker running while I negotiated for a new vehicle. Within an hour, I drove off the lot with a new car. No more pushing, and no more embarrassment.

It is God's will for you to be blessed in every area of life. Wherever you are in your present situation, learn to cast down the thoughts that are holding you back from being blessed. God desires for His people to see themselves the way He does and to receive His best by living in obedience to His Word.

If ye be willing and obedient, ye shall eat the good of the land.

Isaiah 1:19

Don't speak of negative imaginations that you have received from outside sources. Throw them down, pull them down, wrestle them down, cast them down. Put your foot on their neck and say, "That is not me. That is not where I am going. That is not what I am going to do or be. I refuse to live the lifestyle being submitted to me. I take that thought captive now in the name of Jesus." Get violent with the negative thoughts that Satan is submitting to your mind. God has miracles waiting for you. Don't get used to the way things are. They can change for you.

Proverbs 19:21 says:

There are many devices in a man's heart; nevertheless the counsel of the Lord, that shall stand.

God will allow us to receive second best if that is what we desire and want. But we don't have to settle for second best in any part of our lives. Remember this, whatever we receive from Satan, even though it is his best, it is always second best to what God has planned for us. If you catch hold of this principle, you will receive something that will change your life. You will never be the same again or think the way you have been thinking any more. You will think differently, with better thoughts.

Let's compare 2 Corinthians 10:5 with Genesis 6:5-6:

Casting down imaginations, and every high thing that exalteth itself against the knowledge of God, and bringing into captivity every thought to the obedience of Christ.

2 Corinthians 10:5

And God saw that the wickedness of man was great in the earth, and that every imagination of the thoughts of his heart was only evil continually.

**And it repented the Lord that he had made man
on the earth, and it grieved him at his heart.**

Genesis 6:5,6

That is the grieving of the Spirit of God. The Holy
Spirit can be described as a gentleman, easily grieved
by disobedience and vain imaginations. He will not
push Himself on anyone. He only desires to work
through willing vessels.

I once watched a man campaigning for office. He
was standing outside a store with campaign pam-
phlets in his hand, waiting for people to come and
go so he could talk to them. To those who were
willing to listen, he would hand them a pamphlet
and share his ideas and suggestions. Some hurried
by, too busy or going their own way too fast. They
couldn't be part of what he was talking about. Others
moseyed on by, but when they saw him, they looked
away trying to ignore that he was there. Still, he
would try to hand them a pamphlet, and they would
walk by without even looking at him. Others would
take his pamphlet and quickly shake his hand. They
were glad to meet him and hear his suggestions.

The Holy Spirit would like to have a moment of
our time. He would really like to have fellowship
with us. Perhaps early in the morning is a great time

to spend time in prayer with the Holy Spirit. The Lord may say: "You need to spend a few minutes with Me. I have some things I want to share with you that will help you with your life, or business." We can just mosey on by in life trying to ignore Him, or we can say: "Okay, Lord, tell me. What do You want me to know? How do You want to lead me?"

God wants friendship and fellowship heart to heart. He wants you to succeed. He knows that you may have a lot of devices (plans) in your heart, but the plan that He has will stand.

Some say that the Holy Spirit went away when the twelve apostles died. Others say that hearing from God was for years ago and not now. All the while the Holy Spirit is here with the plan on how to change our life. It is up to us to receive Him. The man who was campaigning did not say, "If you don't agree with my thoughts or vote for me, I will punch your lights out." He just stood there. To those who were open, he would share his plan. Those who wouldn't never had the opportunity to hear his views.

Learn to cast down your plan, and exalt God's plan in your life. It will stand.

God has many thoughts and ideas for you that are just what you need. The Holy Spirit has many steps for you to take to be successful. His first requirement is for you to be a willing vessel.

4

⌒∘⌒

Pulling Down Strongholds
in Your Mind

Many people need their minds healed for a variety of reasons: perverted or unchecked sexual fantasies or actions, abuse in past relationships, broken promises or marriages, bad business experiences or career decisions bringing images of failure and poor self-worth repeatedly into their minds. They bear emotional scars. These scars can be removed even though they are not instantly wiped away when a person becomes born again. The reason is that this experience does not immediately affect the mind, which is part of the soul.

The soul involves the mind, will, and emotions. You are a three-part person. You are a spirit (made in the image of God) who possesses a soul made up of your mind (intellect), will (which you control), and emotions. You live in a physical body.

As I stated in Chapter 1, your spirit is born again when you accept Jesus as your Lord and Savior. Your body is to be presented as a living sacrifice until it will be glorified when Jesus comes to meet us in the air. (1 Thess. 4:17.) But according to Romans 12:1-2, your mind must be renewed to the Word of God:

> I beseech you therefore, brethren, by the mercies of God, that ye present your bodies a living sacrifice, holy, acceptable unto God, which is your reasonable service.
>
> And be not conformed to this world, but be ye transformed by the renewing of your mind, that ye may prove what is that good, and acceptable, and perfect, will of God.

The decision to renew your mind is one that *you* must make. It is a step that only *you* can take. This step involves learning to cast down negative thoughts you have received through the years and replacing those thoughts with what the Bible says. This is a lifelong process.

Those dealing with scars must be willing to closely examine and finally reject those things not in line with God's Word, casting them down for good.

Research has shown that many prostitutes and child abusers have a history of being abused, leaving them with thoughts of unworthiness and self-condemnation. The past consistently haunts their minds, captivating them with the thoughts of being victimized in a lifestyle they never wanted. While the physical actions of the past may have long since passed, they remain victimized in their minds. Many of these abused people become abusers themselves if the chain is not broken. But through the blood of Jesus Christ, the chain can be broken.

Maybe you or someone you know has been dealing with these types of problems. Understand this. You can learn how to cast down those thoughts that keep you victimized by the power in the blood of Jesus, while breaking the curse of these actions.

God's Thoughts

In Jeremiah 29:11, God says:

For I know the thoughts that I think toward you, saith the Lord, thoughts of peace, and not of evil, to give you an expected end.

What God thinks about us is so much more important than what we or others think. You may think that you are terrible; that you are dirty, unworthy, filthy, that nobody loves you. You may think that you are a mess, and maybe your lifestyle is. You don't have to continue living that way any longer, because that is not what God thinks of you. He thinks, *If I could only get My children to see that I love them. If I could only get them to understand that I care for them.* God doesn't think the way we think.

Look at verse 12:

Then shall ye call upon me, and ye shall go and pray unto me, and I will hearken unto you.

God meets you where you are. Maybe you are broke, totally bankrupt, backslidden, dealing with sickness or disease in your body, or just emerging from a divorce. God is waiting to hear from you, to heal and deliver you. Once you understand that the thoughts that He has for you are of peace, not of evil (adversity, displeasure), to give you an expected end, then you will realize how God really thinks about you.

Forsaking Thoughts

Let the wicked forsake his way, and the unrighteous man his thoughts....

Isaiah 55:7

If you are going to begin to cast down negative imaginations, then some of your thoughts must be forsaken. That may mean that you are going to have to throw out all the religious or worldly junk you have learned in the past. That includes anything that is contrary to the Word of God. If that is the case, so be it. Throw it out and start replacing it with the Word of God as your foundation.

A few years ago I was invited to help organize, preach, and teach at a conference along with other prominent ministers from various backgrounds. These meetings were going to be very different for a pastor I knew well. He was quite involved with a church group that had strong rules about associating outside of his denomination, which is not according to the Word of God. However, he was invited and agreed to come and speak.

This pastor was so tied into his church's traditions that speaking at a church not affiliated with his denomination was very uncomfortable for him. His arrival at the conference was a real culture shock, because he had some very strong preconceived ideas of what to expect. This was one of the first times he had been around Christian people of different or nondenominational backgrounds. It was hard for him to accept what he saw, because he had been taught over 20 years that his denomination was the only true church.

That evening, he preached a powerful message on learning how to change, which he later told me was more about himself and what he was going through at that time. After ministering to those he usually preached against and believed were against him, he was completely amazed. Contrary to his expectations, the welcome was warm with no regard to his affiliation. The only battle was in his own mind, not with any of his Christian brothers and sisters. He never imagined or expected this to happen.

I later learned that immediately after the conference, he took a three-month sabbatical leave from his post as senior pastor to travel the country and find out what else he had been misinformed about. During this excursion he and his wife visited every type of Christ-centered church he could find from coast to coast, searching for truth. He later told of how he visited these churches, some meeting in barns, some meeting in fields, others meeting in beautiful cathedrals and wonderful buildings with people of every race. During his tour he began to realize that what he had imagined about the entire

Body of Christ, based on the opinions of a few, was not true. His thoughts were incorrect. He began to cast them down and replace them with the truth.

He expressed that he discovered that it did not matter who the people were. After a lot of prayer, he decided to do two things. First, he apologized to his entire congregation for the many years of wrong preaching and teaching and asked for their forgiveness. Next, he announced his resignation from his post as senior pastor. That was a couple of bold steps. But he wanted to change, and he decided to make the first steps.

Tradition vs. God's Word

Your own imagination can take you down the wrong path while leading others with you if not constantly checked by the Word of God. In Mark 7:13 Jesus spoke of...

Making the word of God of no effect through your tradition, which ye have delivered: and many such like things do ye.

You can nullify the Word of God by following a lifestyle based on tradition. All the preaching and teaching and studying you have received is rendered void if tradition has first place in your mind and heart over the Word of God.

We must ask ourselves, *What am I doing and why? Is it because of tradition (versus a relationship with God), or habit, or because of what the Word of God says?*

Self-Examination

Examine yourselves, whether ye be in the faith....

2 Corinthians 13:5

We are to consistently be in the mode of self-examination, not self-condemnation. The Word says to examine. Check yourself with the mirror of the Word of God all of the time. James 1:22-25 reads:

But be ye doers of the word, and not hearers only, deceiving your own selves.

For if any be a hearer of the word, and not a doer, he is like unto a man beholding his natural face in a glass [a mirror]:

For he beholdeth himself, and goeth his way, and straightway forgetteth what manner of man he was.

But whoso looketh into the perfect law of liberty, [the Word of God] and continueth therein, he being not a forgetful hearer but a

doer of the work, this man shall be blessed in his deeds.

If you want your deeds to be blessed, then learn to examine yourself, continue in the Word, and be a doer of the Word.

God desires to bless your deeds, but that blessing will always be in relationship with the Word of God being exalted in your life.

Imagination of God

Perhaps your imagination of God is that of an Ebenezer Scrooge, that He is an old man with a long, gray beard, all withered up, just waiting for someone to do something wrong so He can smack them with a club. If that is even close to the way you imagine your heavenly Father, cast down that thought now, because that may very well be the reason your faith is not working. Your faith is being canceled by your doubt of God's desire for you to prosper and succeed.

Your belief about God must be changed before you can begin to cast down any negative thing that exalts itself against the knowledge of God.

The Word War

In Luke 4:18, the Bible says that Jesus came to heal the brokenhearted and to help those who are bruised. Some of us have bruises on our minds. Our minds have not been bruised physically, although some of us have been physically abused, but for a lot of us, it has just been thought processes that have been bruised. The world, Satan, others, and ourselves have caused us to receive bruises in our minds. If we were to take a look in the Spirit at some of our minds and our thinking process, we would see black and blue marks everywhere.

Your ears may have been bombarded with statements like, "I am leaving." "I quit." "You'll never be anything." "It's terminal." "There is no recovery." "This is it, irreconcilable differences." "We'll always be poor." "People like you aren't welcome here." "You're the wrong color or nationality."

We are in a daily *word war* that goes on in our minds. We must begin to defend ourselves. In fact, go forward and get on the offensive in this word war. But know that when you try to take on the enemy, who is a spirit being, through your flesh, you have just handed yourself instant defeat. You can't win fighting that way. Fight you must, but only in the Spirit to guarantee victory.

> (For the weapons of our warfare are not carnal, but mighty through God to the *pulling down of strongholds;*)
>
> Casting down imaginations, and every high thing that exalteth itself against the knowledge of God....
>
> 2 Corinthians 10:4,5

Notice in the fourth verse, the Bible mentions strongholds. Those words describe a fortified thought, a means of hanging onto a way of thinking, contrary to the Word of God. A stronghold really has little to do in this context with something physical. It has to do with the mental thought patterns of the soul (mind, will, and emotions) going on in the mind. Each stronghold is built brick by brick and left to cement together in the mind of the person over a period of time. Each thought serves as another image or brick in the mind, until the thoughts all come together to form a stronghold. I call these strongholds *thought castles* (based on the root Greek meaning of the word). Once formed, and if left alone, they will become a hardened thought process that will withstand almost anything, even the Word of God, if allowed.

Somewhere, someone submitted to your mind the thoughts that make up what you believe. They were built in your mind brick by brick, thought by thought, until they were left to harden into a stronghold.

So then faith cometh by hearing....

Romans 10:17

Whatever you are constantly hearing, you are building faith for. Words are suggestions and images; the suggestions of the world go into your mind as well as the commandments of God's Word. They are planted into your heart and entertained by your thoughts. If you allow them to stay there to be fertilized, fortified, harbored, and protected, they become strongholds. They determine the actions that you take. All Satan has to do is to plant a suggestion, just one thought at a time, to begin to build a stronghold (a thought castle) in your mind. If it is not uprooted as a thought, it will grow into a stronghold, like a fortified castle. This thought castle serves as the protection of the things that exalt themselves the knowledge of God.

Thought castles (strongholds) are impossible to remove through the flesh, because they are instituted by creative spiritual forces opposed to God. But they are not impossible to remove with the weapons of our warfare through God. That is the reason Paul in 2 Corinthians 10:5 spoke about casting down the imaginations before they become a stronghold. While they are just a thought, before they are an action, cast them down.

Some thoughts are secretly hibernated, protected, and guarded in our minds for so long that they take over. It is similar to the greenhouse effect. We have kept them nice and warm with plenty of sunlight. All the suggestions, the negative thoughts, seeds of defeat, failure, secret sins, and poor self-image are in our minds, incubating and growing. They eventually crowd out and stand hard against the knowledge of God and His Word.

I once saw a movie called "The Blob." The blob was a jelly-like creature that began as a small object no bigger than a fist. Left alone in the right conditions, it grew and grew. First, it took over the room in the house where it was being stored. Then, while being left unchecked, it took over the entire house. It continued and took over the neighborhood. Finally, it overran the city. That is when everyone in the city realized it was a problem, but it was too late. It had grown too big to handle.

"The Blob" is a silly movie, but it is an appropriate analogy of what happens to thoughts left unchecked in our minds. Imaginations will start to grow if left unchecked. The imaginations of man are either good or evil. God destroyed the earth and all the inhabitants (except Noah and his family) for this very reason: The imagination of their thoughts became continually evil. In Genesis 6:5 the Bible doesn't say that God destroyed these people because of the way they looked or talked or because of who they associated with. They were destroyed because of the imagination of the thoughts of their hearts.

Imagination is so vital in the lives of those in God's creation that God will again have to destroy this whole world because of the same thing: the evil imaginations of the hearts of men.

Exalting the Word of God

As Christians, we must learn to cast down imaginations that are exalted above the Word of God.

And God saw that the wickedness of man was great in the earth, and that every imagination of the thoughts of his heart was only evil continually.

Genesis 6:5

Imaginations left unchecked build strongholds that keep you from God. An unchecked mind, an unchecked heart, and an unchecked spirit will take you down to the level of the world quickly. You can't afford that.

Remember this: Once we are born again, Satan cannot change our spiritual destiny without our permission. The choice is made unless we decide otherwise. But he will continue to do anything to try to torment our minds. Here is a biblical example.

Naaman was a Syrian warrior and a very strong man. He was also a leper. He visited the prophet Elijah to be healed, and Elijah told him to dip in the muddy Jordan River seven times. Elijah told him that when he came out of the water the seventh time, he would be healed. Look at Naaman's response:

But Naaman was wroth, and went away, and said, Behold, I thought, He will surely come out to me, and stand, and call on the name of

the Lord his God, and strike his hand over the
place, and recover the leper.

2 Kings 5:11

I can only imagine what the men around
Naaman were saying: "Sir, cast that thought down if
you want to get healed. Your thought does not
matter now; listen to the word of the prophet of
God and be healed." Finally, Naaman listened and
obeyed and was healed just as the prophet said. If
God says to do it one way, you may be saying, "I
thought God would say that I should do it another
way." Naaman was saying the same thing to himself.
If you want the benefits of what God has and does,
you have to learn how to cast down your thoughts
and do it His way. His way is clearly spelled out in
the Bible.

5

Every High Thing That Exalts Itself

There are two main ways that the knowledge of God can be prevented from being received. The first is by not being acknowledged. If I put a $1,000 bill in the back of this book, and you did not acknowledge that it was real, if you thought it was money from a Monopoly game, you would not try to spend it. That is the same way some people hear the message of the Gospel. They do not acknowledge and receive it for themselves.

The second way the knowledge of God is prevented from being received is by ignorance. Some people just have never heard the message of the good news.

Herod and the Word

Let's look at a graphic example of what happened to someone who exalted himself against the knowledge of God. King Herod had beheaded James, the brother of John. This made him very popular with his followers who enjoyed this type of punishment against Christians. Soon after, King Herod made an excellent speech (in the eyes of the audience) to his people.

> ...their country was nourished by the king's country [they received provision from him].
>
> And upon a set day Herod, arrayed in royal apparel, sat upon his throne, and made an oration [a speech] unto them.
>
> And the people gave a shout, saying, It is the voice of a god, and not of a man.
>
> Acts 12:20-22

King Herod came out wearing all of his fancy apparel. After he finished speaking, the people said, "This is the voice of a god; this is not the voice of a man. This is our god speaking." Herod made the mistake of not saying, "No, I am not God. I am only a man. I am only a king appointed by men." Instead, he allowed himself to be exalted above God in the eyes of the people. Herod neglected to restrain their vain thoughts. He actually allowed himself to be exalted above his followers knowing God. He had been killing Christians for sport and then allowed himself to be exalted as God in the imaginations of the people. Look what happened to him as a result.

And immediately the angel of the Lord smote him, because he gave not God the glory: and he was eaten of worms, and gave up the ghost.

Acts 12:23

This is the king who had just killed James and was planning to kill Peter. He was perhaps saying to himself, *I am great. I am wonderful. I am exciting. Look at me. Listen to me everyone, I will tell you great things.* His speech was so wonderful to the people that the people imagined and exclaimed, "That is God." He did not restrain them but probably thought, *Perhaps I am.* That distorted imagination led to his death.

Let's compare this incident to the present. Even in ministry, the days of the superstar personalities are over. God is to receive the glory for the work being done by the Holy Spirit in the Name of Jesus. God's will is that every one of the kings, as well as the people all over the world, receive the Word of God and worship the King of kings and Lord of lords.

But the word of God grew and multiplied.

Acts 12:24

The king died, but the Word of God continued to multiply. God is no respecter of persons. (Acts 10:34.) God will confirm His Word in you when you exalt the Word. There is no force that can stop those who are exalting the Word of God. If you are holding up the Word of God in your thoughts, in your heart, and in your lifestyle, then God is with you. Your enemies may be rising up against you, but you will flourish, because of the Word of God in your life. The Word of God will act as a floatation device to keep you on top no matter what the enemy tries to do to you. So, the Word grew and multiplied, and the king went down in worms.

Anyone who comes against those exalting the Word of God is a fool. The Word will continue and continue and continue to grow!

How Do We See God?

For I say, through the grace given unto me, to every man that is among you, not to think of himself more highly than he ought to think; but to think soberly, according as God hath dealt to every man the measure of faith.

Romans 12:3

Your thinking process, whether negative or positive, good or bad, has to do with your faith. Remember how the children of Israel built a god from their own imagination? What did they build? A calf! The calf was the graven image of their imagination of God. They had seen all the mighty miracles that God had done, yet their imagination of God and His provision was manifested in a golden cow. This was the image of what they could see, in a fleshly sense, from their own idea of what God was to them. Many of us have graven images of God in our mind.

In America, some people, due to some paintings and pictures, imagine Jesus as having blond hair and blue eyes. However, Jewish children are often shocked when they come to America for the first time and see pictures of Jesus with blond hair and blue eyes. Jesus was a Jew, so His appearance was probably not the way Americans imagine Him to be. We must be careful in every area of life not to give impressions by presenting images of our own imaginations of who God is and who He is not.

Look at Paul as he teaches some superstitious people of Athens.

> Forasmuch then as we are the offspring of God, we ought not to think that the Godhead is like unto gold, or silver, or stone, graven by art and man's device.
>
> And the times of this ignorance God winked at; but now commandeth all men every where to repent.
>
> Acts 17:29,30

It is perhaps time for us to change the images we have made of God in our minds. Many people have formed an image of what God happens to be or looks like according to the imaginations of their mind. Unfortunately, that sometimes stifles their freedom to see God as a God for all people and limits their own potential of what they can do in Christ.

6

Bringing Into Captivity Every Thought

Words are actually thought pictures. There is the saying that a picture is worth a thousand words, but I believe that one word can be worth a thousand pictures. When you read these next statements, you will begin to imagine some things.

Dog. Certainly when you read that, you don't just imagine the letters "d-o-g." You see a dog. Each person who reads this will imagine a different kind of dog, but we all see a dog.

Let's be more specific: a black, curly-haired, floppy-eared dog. Do you see him in your mind? As you read the description of the dog, you had to dismiss your imagination and thoughts to put in the thoughts given to you. That is what Satan tries to do. He wants to replace the images of who God desires for you to be with his own words to present another image to you.

There is nothing necessarily wrong with the words I gave you. But words form an image and vision in your mind, and those thoughts must be captured, analyzed, and checked with the Word of God as we have seen in 2 Corinthians 10:5.

If the words are not captured and checked, you may incubate or hibernate the wrong seeds of imagination in the comfortable soil of your mind. They will grow to become a part of your life that you do not want. Every thought is to be your prisoner until you interrogate it as to its origin and purpose and motive with the Word of God.

> For the word of God is quick [alive] and powerful [full of power], and sharper than any twoedged sword, piercing even to the dividing asunder of the soul [mind, will, and emotions] and spirit [human spirit], and the joints and marrow [flesh or body], and is a discerner of the thoughts and intents of the heart.
>
> Hebrews 4:12

Learn to cut your thoughts open with the Word of God. Capture those thoughts, examine them, then either reject or protect them.

The Whirlwind of Instability

There is what I call a whirlwind (tornado) that goes on in some of our minds. Whirlwinds are spawned when hot and cold air come together. When hot and cold air collide in the right conditions, a whirlwind is started. Given a chance to gain momentum, a whirlwind will grow to be a storm of terrific force, and anything that gets in the middle of this hot and cold air is going to be changed, usually negatively.

Some of us have a whirlwind going on in our minds. Everything is confused and seems to be hitting the walls of our mind. Nothing is tied down, nothing is stable. We go from relationship to relationship, from church to church, from thought to thought, from job to job; hot then cold, always finding something wrong with someone or something else—if not the past, then the present, if not the present, then the future. We are not pleased with our jobs, our families, or any of our situations in life. We spawn a state of constant unstableness and confusion all around us. Inside, we are sick with that unstable feeling of uncertainty because of our own imagination. James 1:8 says:

A double-minded man is unstable in all his ways.

Look carefully at this Scripture. It is not his ways that are making this man's mind unstable, but his double-mindedness. Unstable ways are the result of double-mindedness, hot then cold coming together regarding the Word of God. That is the way of the world, not of God.

Stress, depression, worry, or fear in the life of Christians are all due to a double-minded way of thinking. On one hand, the person sees and hears the Word of God and gets excited; then old thoughts and imaginations of the past, fears of the future, or circumstances or situations, begin to crowd out faith in the Word. The person begins to vacillate between fear and faith—hot then cold, cold then hot. Fear of circumstances and situations entering your mind will nullify your faith. If not cast down immediately, they will render the Word of God useless.

Some people allow their imaginations to go so wild that you can see the result on their faces in the form of expressions of worry, fear, grief, hurt, or disappointment. A person's countenance reveals what is going on within him. You can also see joy, peace, and happiness. This is the one area that God cannot control. It's up to you to rise up and take control of this area. You can put a halt on the whirlwind in your mind any time you want to according to the Word of God, with the help of the Holy Spirit.

Taking Control of Thoughts

You will learn how to cast down negative thoughts with a five-step process outlined in the last chapter of this book. But to do this, you must present yourself just as you are and start taking control right where you are in life. "For as he thinketh in his heart, so is he..." (Prov. 23:7). That puts you in control. This is so exciting, because you can change your thought process anytime you want. You can stop thinking on nonproductive imaginations today.

In my early years as a Christian, I was always trying to make my life work my way, while trying to figure out where I was going and what I was supposed to do. No one ever told me that I needed to get my mind renewed to the Word of God or that I needed to start renewing my thoughts. No one ever told me I could cast down the negative thoughts I was entertaining. However, later I discovered in the

Bible that I could renew my mind and cast down the thoughts captivating me.

Mind science and the theory of mind over matter does not work in God's system. It must always be the Word of God and faith over every situation to have consistent victory.

This is a Scripture that you need to underline in your Bible and study:

> **For I know the thoughts that I think toward you, saith the Lord, thoughts of peace [not the tornado, not the confusion], and not of evil, to give you an expected end.**
>
> **Jeremiah 29:11**

We are created to expect something. Begin to expect to receive something good; get a vision for something happening in your life based on the Word of God. We should always be ready to receive whatever God has for us. Expect to receive blessings from God when you pray. This is to be your "expected end." There is nothing or no one that can stop you from being the best you can be. There is nothing to stop you, but you. God is not trying to, and the devil doesn't have the power to, unless you let him. That leaves you in control.

Now unto him that is able to do exceeding abundantly above all that we ask or think, according to the power that worketh in us.

Ephesians 3:20

Start thinking higher thoughts in God.

Research has proven that we use only about 10 percent of our brain capability. Scientists believe that the average person is capable of speaking 200 languages fluently. You have a lot of potential with the Word of God and the Spirit of God working in you.

I decided before I was married that the word *divorce* would not be in my vocabulary. In the early part of our marriage, my wife and I got into a heated "I'm-going-to-leave-and-go-to-my-mother's-house-to-live" discussion. Her mother lived in California, 1,000 miles away, but my wife packed up everything and put it in her car. She put our oldest daughter, Monet (then two years old), in her car seat and drove out of the driveway. I said, "Okay. Have fun at your mother's house."

Neither Kathy nor I wanted this to happen. As she drove off, I said, "I'll be here when you come back." She really didn't want to go to her mother's. She didn't want to go anywhere. She really wanted me to change the way I was acting, and rightfully so. She was making a point: "I'm upset, and you should know it."

I quickly got into my car and tried to follow her. I spotted her driving downtown. She saw me and went over the railroad tracks with the baby's head bouncing as she made her getaway. This went on for about 15 minutes all over the downtown section of our city until Kathy finally stopped, and we began to talk about what was really bothering her. Within a few minutes, we ended up laughing about the whole thing. It was one of the funniest scenes ever.

It is important to deal quickly with the thoughts going on deep down inside of us. My wife had thoughts in her mind, and we had situations that needed to be dealt with and reconciled. There are other thoughts that we cannot allow to occupy space in our minds at all, because if planted in the proper environment, they will cause a world of problems. We should not waste our brain power on these negative thoughts. We must learn to throw them out to be successful in life. If you will consciously say to yourself, "That thought is not according to the will and the purpose of God for me, so I cast it down," your thoughts will begin to change. The only way to do this, as I have said, is by knowing what the Word of God says.

Think on These Things

Finally, brethren, whatsoever things are true, whatsoever things are honest, whatsoever things are just, whatsoever things are pure, whatsoever things are lovely, whatsoever things are of good report; if there be any virtue, and if there be any praise, think on these things.

Phillipians 4:8

Some of us dwell on negative reports; it's our lifestyle. Actually, our minds are occupied by something all of the time, so why not think on the good rather than the bad? We know that there are negative reports, and we are not going to close our eyes to the problems and things that need to be dealt with. But we were not created to keep all the problems of the world in our mind.

Casting down imaginations begins when you first throw down the things that you would normally think and begin inserting the things that God thinks. To think truly great thoughts, we must think the God-kind of thoughts, which are expressed in

God's book, the Bible. Forsake your thoughts, get hold of God's thoughts, and you will be able to do greater things. You must allow new thoughts to be birthed into your heart and mind.

Saturate yourself with the Word of God and watch the seeds grow inside of you as you give place to the birthing process of new ideas according to the will of God. To complete the process, you must plant the Word of God in every area where the evil thoughts have been cast out. The next chapter outlines a five-step CDI (casting down imaginations) process on how to do just that. This process is designed to help you win in every situation in life by utilizing the Word of God. Once you begin to cast down negative imaginations and start exalting the knowledge of God, He is going to give you a new vision. Start this process today. You will see yourself doing something different, exciting, and fruitful.

7

⌒∘⌒

The Five-Step CDI Process

Outlined in this final chapter is a five-step process designed to help you win in every battle or situation in your daily life. It will help change your lifestyle from defeat, fear, complacency, and stagnation by utilizing the Word of God, prayer, and the direction of the Holy Spirit to cast down imaginations and exalt the Word of God.

STEP 1
Receiving

As we have already learned, the first step is receiving. You must be ready to receive those ideas, thoughts, or suggestions that line up with God's will and purpose for your life according to His Word. You must also be ready to reject and cast down those ideas, thoughts, or suggestions that can be detrimental to your growth as a Christian. Your first step in the CDI process is to receive. You will receive information all of the time, but you can control what you receive.

For example, television is one of the most exciting tools the Body of Christ has available to spread the Gospel, which is being preached on certain channels at certain times. However, on some channels you would find programs that are not desirable for a Christian to watch at all. The choice of what you receive is dependent on what channel you choose to tune in on your receiver. You don't have to stop watching television altogether; just tune into the programs that will benefit your life.

As a born-again believer, you cannot allow fear to stop you from being in a receiving posture. Being ready to receive is vitally important to your growth as a Christian.

Second Timothy 1:7 states, "For God hath not given us the spirit of fear...." Notice, fear is a spirit. You must come against that spirit of fear, bind that spirit of fear, and cast that spirit down out of your mind in order to be ready to freely receive, or the spirit of fear will rule and reign in your life above the knowledge of God.

That verse also says, "For God hath not given us the spirit of fear; but of power, and of love, and of a sound mind."

STEP 2
Analyzing

The second step in the CDI process is analyzing what you have received. For many Christians this step is clouded by the often-asked question: "Analyze what with what?" Second Corinthians 10:5 answers that valid question:

> ... **bringing into captivity every thought to the obedience of Christ.**

Can you see it now?

To be effective in winning the battles you are faced with every day in life, you must capture (make prisoner) every thought (yes, every thought) that comes to your mind and analyze it in comparison to its obedience (or lack of obedience) to God's will in your life, before you act on it.

The Bible states in John 1:14 that Jesus is the Word made flesh. It is up to you to take every thought prisoner, but remember that you must do this. God will not do it for you. He has given you every weapon you need to make wise decisions in every area of life based on His Word. (You, too, must become the Word wrapped in flesh, dwelling on this earth.)

Of all the steps in this five-step process, this one is where many Christians get clouded in their brain, because they don't know what the Word of God says regarding obedience. Most people know only Bible stories and abstract information about the Bible, but many people think it is impossible to know how to live a lifestyle as a Christian according to the Bible. They have not been taught to capture the thoughts of their mind in light of the Word of God. They try to do it from a cultural or worldly view with no reference to the Bible to back up the standards. Simply put, they know the traditions of men, their religious creed, sectarian statements, or cultural beliefs, but they don't truly know the Word of God and how to apply it to their everyday situations. That simply will not work!

The Scripture says, "to the obedience of Christ," and that is what it means. You must be ready to find out what the Bible says about each area you are dealing with, not what Brother so-and-so thinks the

Bible said about that area, or what you thought you heard the preacher say one day about that area. You must know for yourself what the Word of God says about that area, or suggestion, thought, or idea that has been presented to your mind. If you don't know what is in obedience to Christ concerning that thought, then one of two things will result, both equally negative.

Perhaps you will, out of ignorance of the Word of God and fear of exalting the wrong thing, cast down a thought, idea, or suggestion that is in obedience to the Word and miss out on the promises and blessings associated with it. Or you will exalt a negative idea, thought, or suggestion that will pass the analytical test in your mind, and because of ignorance mistake it as being in obedience to Christ. You will then put it into your mind and begin to accept it as a part of your lifestyle. It will be to your detriment simply because of a lack of knowledge of the Word.

In Hosea 4:6 the Lord says:

My people are destroyed for lack of knowledge: because thou hast rejected knowledge, I will also reject thee, that thou shalt be no priest to me: seeing thou hast forgotten the law of thy God, I will also forget thy children.

Your ignorance of the Word of God may be hurting you, your family, and your children.

Part of the training for an FBI counterfeit specialist is first to perfect the study of the pattern and makeup of true, legitimate U.S. currency. This is done long before specialists attempt to compare their knowledge to the discerning of counterfeit bills. Like the FBI, you must first become proficient in knowing the Word of God; then you are ready to rightly divide the Word of God from the lies of the devil submitted to you. If you are unsure about analyzing thoughts, suggestions, or ideas, then determine to learn to rightly divide the Word of truth.

STEP 3
Accepting or Rejecting

The third step is also a crucial pivot point in the entire CDI process. Once you have received and analyzed the information, thought, suggestion, or idea that has been presented to you, you must now do something with it—either accept it or reject it. There is no middle ground about this. Either one or the other will happen, no matter how you try to avoid it. In Revelation 3:15 Jesus said to the angel of the church of Laodicea:

> **I know thy works, that thou art neither cold nor hot: I would thou wert cold or hot.**
>
> **So then because thou art lukewarm, and neither cold nor hot, I will spue [spit] thee out of my mouth.**

You will have to decide if you are cold or hot regarding each idea, thought, or suggestion that is presented to you. You will have to learn how to spew some things out of your mind in order to grow in the things of God; that's just the way it is.

One of the hardest things for Christians to do is to realize they must reject some of the thoughts, suggestions, or ideas from some well-meaning people in their life. Some of these people may be very close, perhaps a close relative or a long-time friend or religious associate who has been suggesting some things that don't line up with the will of God expressed in the Word of God. Rejecting these suggestions at first is very hard, but you must understand that you will have to learn how to be either hot or cold on an idea, suggestion, or thought, all based upon the Word of God. Lukewarm won't do.

As you make your decision, let me help you to see what happens with that idea, thought, or suggestion that you are dealing with by explaining it this way: If it meets the test by analyzing it with the Word of God, normally all rejection efforts will be dropped at that time. It is then accepted and will become a part of the stronghold (another brick in building a fortified wall) as you protect that part of your lifestyle, knowing its foundation is the Word. Over time, that accepted thought or idea will become a part of the wall protecting a part of your lifestyle, thoughts, morals, and actions.

The sad part about this process is that many Christians with a lack of knowledge of the Word of God become stifled with the negative ideas, thoughts, or suggestions they have accepted over the years. They receive undesirable results, because what they are exalting is not according to the Word. Over time, as these people build strongholds in their minds, those negative, untrue thoughts, ideas, and suggestions become exalted over the truth of God's Word, making it of no effect. And they become hardened and fortified, just as though they were the Word of God.

This process (accepting or rejecting) is really not new at all; it has been going on since the Creation. However, many Christians don't seem to know that they can be victorious in this process in their daily lives. Every believer has been given authority over this area in the Name of Jesus. However, you must use God's weapons to be successful in tearing down these strongholds. Your weapon is the sword of the Spirit, the Word of God. (Eph. 6:17.)

Your physical efforts won't work. Our weapons of warfare aren't carnal, and we must cast down imaginations. (2 Cor. 10:4,5.) You see, the only way you can know how to cast down thought castles (strongholds) in your mind is through God, not through any carnal or fleshly means. Trying to do this in the flesh or in your own power is like trying to break down a physical brick wall with your bare hands. It is impossible without using the right tools. God knows you'll need a spiritual jackhammer, a sledgehammer, a bulldozer, and a wrecking ball to make the needed changes in your life. He has all that you need to cast down the negative thought castles in your mind and reestablish the Word in its place.

I like to explain it this way. To get things on the right track, you must be willing to take out the weapons that God has given you to cast down those thoughts that you are holding on to (maybe secretly) by rejecting those things that do not meet the standards of a lifestyle based on the Word of God. Next, be ready to exalt the Word of God in that area, tearing down that old thought in comparison with the living Word of God.

Here's a practical suggestion: Make a point to take time to sit down with a piece of paper and a pencil or pen and examine yourself, writing down changes that you need to make. Be ready to accept or reject some of your ways and protected thoughts in light of the Word of God. Do this before you move on to expand into any new ground in your life. Remember, you must do this with the willingness to change, or it will do no good at all.

STEP 4
Replacing

After the first three steps in the CDI process, you probably feel as if you are making progress. Perhaps you have discovered and cast down some things you may have been thinking about yourself or others that were not right, or maybe something you were doing that was not according to the Word of God, and these things have now been cast down, repented of, and removed. Though these are bold and noble steps, stopping now will only ensure eventual defeat. This is where most Christians get stagnated in their Christian life. They have completed all the don'ts but know nothing about the do's. Step 4, replacing, will ensure that you will continue to grow as a Christian and continue to change as you receive God's promises.

Before we explore this area, you must decide in your mind that living daily as a Christian is the type of lifestyle you want beginning today, and for the remainder of your life. Casting negative thoughts, ideas, and suggestions out of your mind is one thing, but you can't operate your life on emptiness, vacancy, or in a rejection state. Someday you are going to have to occupy that space with something that is positive and according to the will of God to win. As a child of God, you must be ready to replace old thoughts, ideas, and suggestions with God's Word.

Let's review. Once the thought or idea is received, it is analyzed. When that thought is analyzed and found not to meet the standards in the Word of God, it is then rejected, and that empty place must be filled with the Word of God. Learn now to remember to replace each negative thought, idea, or suggestion with the Word of God that you used to analyze it. By doing so you allow those Scriptures to become the new standard in your lifestyle in that area for the rest of your life. That becomes your confession of faith. You are confessing God's promises that will come to pass for you in that area.

In Psalm 119:89, the Bible states:

Forever, O Lord, thy word is settled in heaven.

Learn to settle your matters with the Word of God, because the Word of God is already settled. Remembering to replace negative thoughts with the promises of God ensures that you will always keep yourself growing in the Word, settled in the things of God and not the whims of the world's ideas.

STEP 5
Renewing

I beseech you therefore, brethren, by the mercies of God, that ye present your bodies a living sacrifice, holy, acceptable unto God, which is your reasonable service.

And be not conformed to this world, but be ye transformed by the renewing of your mind, that ye may prove what is that good, and acceptable, and perfect, will of God.

Romans 12:1,2

For some Christians, memorizing Scriptures is not a very hard task to accomplish. However, in our final step in the five-step CDI process, we will find that just having head knowledge of the Word of God alone will not change your lifestyle. This is the area that has to do with religion. Many people think that it is a compliment to be called religious.

Being called religious is not a compliment at all. Jesus dealt with many religious leaders of His day. To be religious simply means to continually do the same thing. For example, most people religiously go to work in the morning. Like a ritual, they get up at the same time and do the same things every morning to prepare themselves, day after day, religiously. But, these same people if offered a job across the street paying a little bit more would quit their present job in a moment, because they are not committed to that company, even though they have been doing the same thing day after day, week after week, month after month, year after year, religiously.

They are just religious. Many people treat the Word of God the same way. They recite the same Scriptures with the same lack of faith and get the same old negative results no matter what.

To be successful in growing in the things of God, you must accept the fact that you are to be renewing your mind to the Word of God every day, not just going through a religious routine to be seen of men. When it comes to the CDI process, you can do all of the first four steps and end up frustrated and religious if Step No. 5, renewing your mind, is not included. Learn to renew your mind. Meditate and observe. It is not enough just to know the Word of God, but your lifestyle must be known by doing the Word of God. Become a living example of God's Word in your life, your word and your deed. It's your decision.

You can become victorious and more effective for the kingdom of God by learning to cast down negative thoughts and exalting the Word of God. Decide today to: **Step 1** *Receive;* **Step 2** *Analyze;* **Step 3** *Reject or Accept (cast down or fortify);* and **Step 4** *Replace (with the Word of God);* and **Step 5** *Renew Your Mind.* My life and the lives of many others have completely changed, and so can yours as you begin this daily process.

Prayer of Salvation

God loves you—no matter who you are, no matter what your past. God loves you so much that He gave His one and only begotten Son for you. The Bible tells us that "...whoever believes in him shall not perish but have eternal life" (John 3:16 NIV). Jesus laid down His life and rose again so that we could spend eternity with Him in heaven and experience His absolute best on earth. If you would like to receive Jesus into your life, say the following prayer out loud and mean it from your heart.

Heavenly Father, I come to You admitting that I am a sinner. Right now, I choose to turn away from sin, and I ask You to cleanse me of all unrighteousness. I believe that Your Son, Jesus, died on the cross to take away my sins. I also believe that He rose again from the dead so that I might be forgiven of my sins and made righteous through faith in Him. I call upon the name of Jesus Christ to be the Savior and Lord of my life. Jesus, I choose to follow You and ask that You fill me with the power of the Holy Spirit. I declare that right now I am a child of God. I am free from sin and full of the righteousness of God. I am saved in Jesus' name. Amen.

If you prayed this prayer to receive Jesus Christ as your Savior for the first time, please contact us on the web at www.harrisonhouse.com to receive a free book.

Or you may write to us at
Harrison House
P.O. Box 35035
Tulsa, Oklahoma 74153

About the Author

Donald Shorter was born in New Orleans, Louisiana, to Pastor Roosevelt and Mary Shorter, and at the age of 12, Don was born again and accepted his call to ministry at the age of 18. While attending Lincoln High School in Tacoma, Washington, he met a beautiful young lady, the former Kathy Lynette Hill, who later became his wife in July 1974.

Upon completion of college, Dr. Shorter embarked upon a highly successful secular radio and television broadcasting career as a television host on the Seattle, Washington ABC affiliates. However, his call to the ministry remained the impetus in his life, and in January 1987, with his family of four, Pastor Shorter founded Pacific Christian Center Church.

Dr. Shorter received his masters in business administration in 1993, was ordained by Dr. Frederick K. C. Price in 1994, and received his doctorate of ministry in 1999. Each of these events has played a significant role in his success as a pastor.

Today, under the oversight of Dr. Don and Kathy Shorter, Pacific Christian Center is a worldwide ministry that ministers to thousands each week through speaking engagements, radio and television broadcasts, regular church services, and business seminars. Through their teaching and faith-based outreaches, such as Real Dads in America, Kathy's Kids, Excellence in Business, Men of Excellence, and Women of Wealth, the Shorters touch many lives.

Dr. and Mrs. Shorter are the parents of three children—Monet, Dawnet, and Donald Jr.

Other Books by Dr. Donald Shorter

Casting Down Imaginations

The Power in You

Books by Kathy Shorter

Desperate Dieters

Guard Your Heart

Heaven Yes! Hell No!

To contact Dr. Shorter, write to:

Dr. Donald Shorter

P.O. Box 44800 • Tacoma, WA 98444

or to:

Pacific Christian Center Church

3211 112th Street East • Tacoma, WA 98446

(253)-536-0801

or visit him on the web at:

www.pacificchristiancenter.org

Additional copies of this book are
available from your local bookstore.